The state of Kansas, right in the
center of the United States, is far
from any ocean. Farmland and
cities flourish on a broad plain.
But travel back 82 million years,
and the scene is very different.
There are no cities.
There are no farms.
There are no people.

And the animals . . .

Well, this is the Mesozoic era,
and dinosaurs rule the land.

Flying reptiles soar on their great
wings above both land and sea.
And in the inland sea that covered
the whole middle of North America
prowl more giant predators.

The largest and most ferocious is *Tylosaurus*.
As long as a school bus, it has eyes as big as grapefruit
and rows of cone-shaped teeth.
And *Tylosaurus* is just one of the many
prehistoric reptiles we call . . .

SEA MO

A PREHISTORI

Marfé Ferguson Delano

BASED ON THE GIANT-SCREEN FILM WRITTEN BY
Mose Richards

Funded in part by the National Science Foundation

NATIONAL GEOGRAPHIC
WASHINGTON, DC

Funded in part by the National Science Foundation

Photo of Kansas, p. 1: Mark Thiessen/ National Geographic Giant Screen Films
Photo of *Dolichorynchops* skeleton, p. 32: Rocky Mountain Dinosaur Resource Center

Paperback ISBN: 978-1-4263-0162-9
Library edition ISBN: 978-1-4263-0119-3
Cataloging in Publication Data available upon request.

Printed in Mexico

Founded in 1888, the National Geographic Society is one of the largest nonprofit scientific and educational organizations in the world. It reaches more than 285 million people worldwide each month through its official journal, NATIONAL GEOGRAPHIC, and its four other magazines; the National Geographic Channel; television documentaries; radio programs; films; books; videos and DVDs; maps; and interactive media. National Geographic has funded more than 8,000 scientific research projects and supports an education program combating geographic illiteracy.

For more information, please call 1-800-NGS LINE (647-5463) or write to the following address:

NATIONAL GEOGRAPHIC SOCIETY
1145 17th Street N.W., Washington, D.C. 20036-4688 U.S.A.

Visit us online at www.nationalgeographic.com/books

For information about special discounts for bulk purchases, please contact
National Geographic Books Special Sales: ngspecsales@ngs.org

For rights or permissions inquiries, please contact National Geographic Books Subsidiary Rights: ngbookrights@ngs.org

NATIONAL GEOGRAPHIC GIANT SCREEN FILMS PRESENTS SEA MONSTERS: A PREHISTORIC ADVENTURE NARRATED BY LIEV SCHREIBER
EXECUTIVE MUSIC PRODUCER PETER GABRIEL ORIGINAL SCORE BY RICHARD EVANS DAVID RHODES AND PETER GABRIEL SOUND DESIGN MICHAEL STEARNS PRODUCTION DESIGN CHAS. BUTCHER
DIRECTORS OF PHOTOGRAPHY T.C. CHRISTENSEN BOB CRANSTON EDITED BY JONATHAN SHAW EXECUTIVE PRODUCER TIM KELLY PRODUCED BY LISA TRUITT JINI DURR WRITTEN BY MOSE RICHARDS DIRECTED BY SEAN MACLEOD PHILLIPS

www.nationalgeographic.com/seamonsters

Compared to the deep sea, the shallow waters near the shore are safe. That's where this *Dolichorynchops osborni* ("dolly" for short) has come to give birth.

Baby dollies are born underwater and are only about 18 inches (46 cm) long at birth. This newborn pair heads to the surface to take their first breaths of air.

The young dollies and their mother are only a few of the animals that live in the shallows. They share their neighborhood with some pretty amazing creatures.

The giant turtle *Protostega* weighs about a ton. That's 2,000 pounds (900 kg). When it's time for her to lay her eggs, she has to pull that huge body up onto the beach.

There are ammonites hunting the shallows. Their rock-hard spiral shells protect their soft bodies from predators.

The strangest of the young dollies' neighbors is their distant cousin *Styxosaurus*. More than half its length is just neck—a perfect tool for nabbing a fish dinner.

CAPROBERYX

As the young female dolly and her twin brother begin to grow up, they master the art of catching their food. A *Caproberyx* is always a nice treat.

TUSOTEUTHIS

In the deep water they encounter animals they have
never seen before. This is a *Tusoteuthis,* a 35-foot
(10-meter) animal similar to the giant squid of today.

Some new neighbors seem less than friendly. When a school of *Xiphactinus* fish zoom in their direction, the dollies get out of the way fast. These minivan-size fish with razor-sharp teeth swallow their victims whole.

But escape is not always possible, and one day our dolly family is attacked by sharks. A *Cretoxyrhina*, as big as the great white shark of our day, swoops in and seizes the mother dolly in its deadly jaws. She dies quickly, a meal for a monster.

ENCHODUS

Another favorite is a fish called *Enchodus* that swims in swirling schools. When the *Enchodus* schools begin their annual migration, the dolly family and many of their neighbors follow their food out into the deeper waters of the inland sea.

A small shark has bitten the young female dolly's flipper. Confused by her mother's violent end, she doesn't realize at first that she has been attacked. She will always carry a reminder of her close call—a shark tooth stuck in her flipper.

Life goes on, even after a shark attack. On their own now, the young dollies hurry to keep up with the *Enchodus* school and eventually join another group of dollies.

The migration continues. Avoiding predators as best they can, the dollies encounter the wonders of the Mesozoic sea. Drifting schools of jellyfish shimmer in the water. At night, microscopic plankton give off an eerie glow.

But danger is never very far away. A giant *Tylosaurus* sneaks up on the dollies . . .

. . . and swallows the brother whole!

The *Tylosaurus* that ate the brother dolly is full and slow moving. He may be the ruler of the seas, but he, too, has enemies. Sensing his momentary weakness, a larger, stronger *Tylosaurus* is about to attack.

Injured and weighed down by his meal of dolly, the first *Tylosaurus* will sink to the sea floor and be devoured by hungry sharks.

The last of her family, the female dolly swims away with the group.

The dolly migration continues, and the female dolly's luck holds. She survives her first season in the world of sea monsters and returns to the shallows. After several seasons, she starts a family of her own.

Her youngsters will grow strong in the sheltered shallows. Then one day, they will set out on their own journey—to the realm of sea monsters, the vast inland sea.

And what about the mother? She will live a long life and eventually die of old age. Her body will drift to the sea floor, where her bones will slowly turn to stone.

Millions of years later,

when the sea is gone

and the land is part of the vast plains of Kansas,

paleontologists will find our dolly

and figure out her story.

For Elise Neilson ~ J.W.

For Jonse and Karen, who have monstrously good hair ~ J.D.

tiger tales

5 River Road, Suite 128, Wilton, CT 06897

Published in the United States 2018

Originally published in Great Britain 2018

by Little Tiger Press

Text copyright © 2018 Jeanne Willis

Illustrations copyright © 2018 Jenni Desmond

ISBN-13: 978-1-68010-077-8

ISBN-10: 1-68010-077-7

Printed in China

LTP/1400/1975/0917

All rights reserved

10 9 8 7 6 5 4 3 2 1

For more insight and activities, visit us at www.tigertalesbooks.com

by

JEANNE WILLIS

illustrated by

JENNI DESMOND

RAAAR

BLUE
MONSTER
WANTS
IT ALL!

tiger tales

Blue Monster loved brand-new things more than anything.

When he was a baby, he said,
"I don't want my old buggy.
I want a new one!"

He wouldn't stop screaming
until he got it.
But . . .

...it didn't make him happy for long.

"I don't want my old teddy bear!" he said.

"I want something new to cuddle!"

And he threw it out of the buggy.

So ...

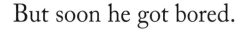

... his mom and dad gave him a baby sister. Blue Monster loved cuddling her at first.

But soon he got bored.

"I don't want my old sister!" he yelled.
"I don't want my old teddy bear!
Or my old mom and dad!"

He took all the money his grandma had given him and left home to start a new life.

Blue Monster bought himself a new hat.

He liked it so much,
he wore it all morning.
But that afternoon
he said . . .

..."I don't want this old hat!
I want something new!"
He stamped his hat flat
and bought ...

a shiny red sports car.
He loved his new car.

BEEP

But the next day, Blue Monster didn't like it one bit.
"I don't want my old car!" he screamed. "I want to buy
a great big golden palace with a carnival and a circus!"

Which he did. And it was wonderful. But only
for a while. "What I really need is a new . . ."

…"airplane!" said Blue Monster. So he
bought a jumbo jet and flew off…

... to a tropical island near New Guinea.
"This looks like paradise!" said Blue Monster.
So he bought the entire island and
everything on it. But ...

... he didn't want the old animals who
lived there. So he bought new gorillas,
new polar bears,
new zebras, and ...

a new submarine,
so he could watch
his new whales.

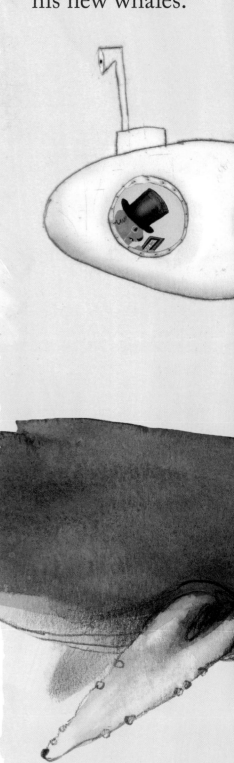

That night, he climbed into his
new hammock.

"I've bought everything I need
to make me happy now," he smiled.
Then he drifted off to sleep beneath
the stars.

Blue Monster woke up to a brand-new day.
His new birds were singing. His new bees
were buzzing. The sun was shining,
but he still wasn't happy.

"I don't want that old sun!"
he said. "I want a new one!"

So he snatched it out of the sky. And
he ATE it! Everything went dark.

Blue Monster was cold and scared and alone.
He really needed a hug, but none of his
new things could comfort him.

"Never mind,"
he sniffed. "I'll go and
buy myself a new . . ."

"...family!"

But there are some things money just can't buy.

There were no families for sale.

Or friends.

Blue Monster began to sob. He sobbed
so hard, he spat out the sun.

Suddenly, he saw the light.
"I don't *need* a new family!"
he cried. "I love . . ."

"…my old family!"

So Blue Monster fixed his broken plane
and flew all the way home …

... to give his old mom, his old dad, and his old sister a good old hug.
This made Blue Monster feel a hundred times happier than new hats,
fast planes, and a paradise island ever could.

BECAUSE ...

...he had **everything** he could ever need.

RAAAR